Custom Electrical Panels & Wiring Harnesses

ALSO BY ROBIN G. COLES

Boating Secrets: 127 Top Tips to Help You Buy and/or Enjoy Your Boat

Buying a Boat, an Interview w/Captain Chris Kourtakis

Marine Surveys, an Interview w/Rob Scanlan

Insuring a Boat, an Interview w/Mike Smith

Financing a Boat Purchase, an Interview w/Jim Coburn

Rent Your Boat, an Interview w/Brian Stefka

Search and Rescue, an Interview w/Alan Sorum

Bad Storms/Heavy Weather, an Interview w/Timothy Wyand

Digital Selective Calling (DSC), the Automatic Identification System (AIS), and Automated Radio Checks (ARC), an Interview w/Captain Chris Kourtakis

Multihulls, an Interview w/Jim Brown

Custom Electrical Panels and Wiring Harnesses, an Interview w/Mark Rogers

Making a Living as a Professional Sailor, an Interview w/Brian Hancock

Seven Tips for a Successful Sale of Your Used Boat

4 Essential Steps to Buying Your Boat

Or, go to: Boating Secrets Website (BoatingSecrets127TopTips.com) for all our books, audios, and transcripts

Custom Electrical Panels & Wiring Harnesses

An Interview with Mark Rogers

Robin G. Coles

TheNauticalLifestyle.com

Custom Electrical Panels & Wiring Harnesses: An Interview with Mark Rogers

Copyright © 2012 Robin G. Coles

www.TheNauticalLifestyle.com
ISBN: 098363811X
ISBN-13: 978-0-9836381-1-7

Dedication

For my aunt, Ruth Shoer, who passed away before this book was finished.

I miss you!

"Why Haven't Boat Owners Been Told These Facts Before?"

Karen G. Coles
TheMarineSafetyteam.com

You already know buying a boat is one of the most challenging things you'll ever do in your life. And, it's an awesome way to include both your family and friends. Not to mention all the fun you'll have out on the water. But, do you know the...

✔ Do's and don'ts when buying a boat

✔ Two little known tools surveyors use to determine a boat's age and condition

✔ Three surprising reasons why marinas require the insurance they do

✔ How you can still get a boat loan even if your credit score is less than 720

✔ How a commercial emergency signaling technology has saved more than 25,000 lives since 1982 and is now available for pleasure boaters

✔ What to do when you get caught in a bad storm or heavy weather

✔ Why customizing your electrical and instrument panels makes sense

✔ How Digital Selective Calling and the Automated Identification System saves lives in a Search and Rescue Operation

✔ The advantages and disadvantages of having a multihull craft over a monohull

✔ Three powerful strategies you can use to best prepare your boat for rentals

✔ What's changed to take sailing from an amateur sport to top of the game earning a decent living

Now imagine having eleven of the top marine industry experts sitting with you and spilling all of these secrets plus more. Well... now you can!

Introducing...

A complete guide for new and seasoned boaters to buy and enjoy your boat

Boating Secrets
*127 Top Tips to Help You Buy and Enjoy Your Boat,
Revealed by Eleven Marine Industry Experts
Vol. I)*

Boating Secrets Testimonials

Robin Coles has impressed me very much as a friend and an advocate to the marine industry. Her website TheNauticalLifestyle.com has become a work of "internet art" for the average boater.

I listened to her discussions with industry experts that are the basis for her book and was totally impressed at the quality of her participating experts, their knowledge and Robin's ability to ask the right questions, as well as her follow up questions.

Anyone seeking to purchase a new boat or intending to buy a larger boat should have her book in their library.

Captain Leo Corsetti, Arlington, MA, Retired, Tone President,
Proud Tartan Owner

~~~

Robin Coles has done a wonderful job of covering a comprehensive list of topics that will help new and experienced boaters get the most out of their investment.

An educated boater is a better boater and a better boater is much more likely to enjoy a lifetime of fun with family and friends.

Robin taps into many of the recreational boating industry's most experienced experts who will help you avoid many of the situations that inexperienced boaters could find themselves in. A boat is a significant investment of your time in an era where free time is much harder to come by.

This Nautical Lifestyle Expert Series is sure to help you maximize your investment while making you a better captain when you inevitably find yourselves in harrowing situations. As the captain, you take on huge responsibilities and it's important that boating safety is always top of mind. It may save your life or one of your loved ones.

Carl Blackwell, Vice President, Discover Boating,
National Marine Manufacturers Association (NMMA)

Contents

Author's Introduction

So why am I writing or, more to the point, why did I make this interview series into a book?

Not everyone likes to listen or learns by listening. Some of us still like holding a book in our hands, feeling the weight of it on our laps, and even going through it page by page with a highlighter and marking what's important to us as we read. I'm one of those rare birds who still likes to hold a book and feel its weight in the crook of my arm while I have a good cup of tea. Others nowadays are reading books on their computers or even on Amazon's Kindle or Barnes and Noble's NOOK. Who knows? There might even be something new by the time you read this. I also find that a reference book, which this certainly could be, is great when it's accessible on your book shelf—you can quickly thumb through it to find the information you're looking for. You could add a different colored sticky note to the first page of each chapter for quick reference.

Others learn by listening, and that's great too! But I wanted to make sure I had this book in different media for everybody. That's how important I believe this project is. It's important because for years now, as I've learned more and more about boating, I've found there isn't a lot of basic information out there; and the information that I can find is scattered all over the place. Also, I'm not always sure of the credentials of the people writing articles about boating.

But, let's back up a few years and start at the beginning.

Growing up, I always had a fascination for the ocean and the skies—the moon and the stars. At night I would watch the moon follow me around and search the sky for the big dipper, little dipper, Hercules, and other constellations. When I was a little girl, my aunt Dee would take me to Revere Beach and we would walk the beach. She never let me go into the water without shoes on my feet for fear of seaweed wrapping around my legs and pulling me under. (What wearing shoes had to do with that, I'm not sure.) So I never went into the water, but always dreamed about it. When I got my own car I would head to Storrow and Memorial Drives on my lunch breaks and watch the sailboats on the Charles River, wishing it was me on one of them. (I also had a fascination for airplanes—watching them take off and land at airports—but that's another story for another time. Maybe I've just wanted to escape from day-to-day life. I guess that's why I now live near both an airport and the ocean.)

Fast forward to April 5, 2001. I was told over the phone that I had cancer. A couple of days later, in the doctor's office, I was told that I had less than ten years to live. The year before I'd been misdiagnosed with multiple sclerosis and told that I'd be confined to a wheel chair within a year. Doctors can be so cruel in what they tell you and, more importantly, how they tell you. After I came to terms with this news, and after I grieved for the person I once knew and had been, I set out to make some changes in my life. It was time to conquer my fear of being on the ocean. I called a friend of mine and asked him to take me kayaking. He did, and that experience really changed my outlook. Kayaking was so peaceful and fun. If I hadn't almost been hit by a tanker, I probably would have gone again. Of course, I'd also been afraid of tipping over (I'm not a very good swimmer), an odd fear to have surfaced in me since my sons and I had done a lot of canoeing and rowing during our many camping trips when they were young and I hadn't been afraid then.

Next, I took up sailing. I had looked into sailing on the Charles River, but at that school one first had to pass a swim test, which I didn't believe I could do, and I really wanted to learn on the ocean. Ocean sailing was an experience that I found to be the epitome of relaxation. I absolutely fell in love with sailing and couldn't get out into Boston Harbor enough. Mark, my primary sailing instructor, had so much passion both for the sport and for teaching that he made learning to sail really enjoyable. As with everything, some of my instructors were better than others. But Mark was awesome and whenever I went sailing on the 23-foot Sonar, I felt the boat and I were one. I could hop into the cockpit, grab the tiller, and feel her every move as we'd glide through the waves.

One day I went to the Sailing Center with a sailing buddy and we took out a boat with which neither of us was familiar. The boat was six feet longer than what we were used to and it had a steering wheel. I had never sailed a boat with a wheel before, but off we went. This was something new to learn—great! Wrong. Neither of us was experienced with this size or type of boat and we had no business taking it out by ourselves. What happened to us that afternoon would never have happened if we had taken out the 23-foot Sonar instead. We got caught in a couple of wind and rain storms. We tried taking the sails down, but the furlings came off. The wind kept pushing us sideways. I was trying to hold the wheel and watch the skipper on deck to make sure he didn't fall overboard. The wind and rain squall picked up and pushed us right onto the beach—we ended up going aground. Then the engine wouldn't start and we had to call Sea Tow. One of the topics we discuss in this book is heavy weather. A big part of that is knowing your boat, which neither of us did. It was scary.

In 2006, I went to a National Geographic Travel Writing workshop in New York. There I met a woman who also loved sailing and we hung out together for the day. When the workshop was over, she told me that she knew someone who was looking for a reviewer, writer, and photographer for a cruising guide book. She suggested I take a look at the website and then call her if I was interested. I did. A few days later, the publisher called me. That year, after they'd trained me, the project was cancelled. In 2007, the project was on again, so off I went.

My assignment was to review, write about, and photograph over 200 marinas from Block Island, Rhode Island, to St. John's

River in New Brunswick, Canada. I spent three months on the road, staying in hotels, motels, and bed and breakfasts, keeping a ridiculous schedule in order to get that project done. One thing I learned along the way is that boaters are a very friendly group. There's a different mindset when you're on the water versus being in the corporate grind every day. I liked it. For a number of other reasons, this project turned sour and never came to fruition.

But it was during this project that I met Chuck, the local harbormaster, and got to know and work alongside him. It was also during this time that Winthrop, Massachusetts, the town I'd just moved back to, was putting in a new marina. There were lots of questions being asked, and speculations being made, by the townspeople about the new marina. I approached Chuck the following spring and we did an interview which I recorded and put up on the web. This interview answered a lot of questions for the residents and the project continued with fewer objections. For a while after that I wrote a weekly column for the local newspaper reporting on activities at the local marinas and yacht clubs.

Around that time I started studying marketing on the internet with Mark Hendricks. I needed something to work on and decided to take everything I'd learned during the project from hell and turn it into something positive. This new project became TheNauticalLifestyle.com and it is always evolving. I'm not afraid to try something new and if it sticks, great. If not, why not?

One thing I learned during both projects is that I love interviewing people—I guess it goes with that curious mind of mine. You know how some children are always asking why, why, why? That's me, still to this day—always asking why; always seeking, searching for answers. But it can't be just any answer—it has to make sense.

Content, content, content is what Google looks for and what Mark stresses in his internet marketing lessons. So I posted a request on LinkedIn indicating that I was looking for speakers for an interview series that I was putting together. The rest, as they say, is history.

In this book I have tried to cover all of the basics as well as some more advanced boating topics for the old salts. It's filled with lots of answers that should enhance your boating experiences. Interviewing these knowledgeable gentlemen has taught me a lot and it's truly been a pleasure working with them. My wish is for you to get just as much out of reading this book as I have in putting it together.

The final reason for creating this book is that as I have ventured out on my journey to become a better boater, I've had many questions. What better way to get them answered than to interview the experts? So that's what I did.

Custom Electrical Panels & Wiring Harnesses

An Interview with Mark Rogers

Introduction

Robin: Hello everyone. This is Robin Coles and it's my pleasure to welcome you to the Nautical Lifestyle Expert Series brought to you by TheNauticalLifestyle.com. In the next hour you're going to learn about custom electrical and instrumental panels along with wiring harnesses. I'm honored to have Mark Rogers as my special guest today. Hello Mark!

Mark: Hi Robin, it's a pleasure talking with you.

Robin: Mark, thank you so much for joining me. Mark started out around 15 years old as a studio engineer at a local radio station. He tried college for a couple of semesters, then joined a band and traveled around the eastern part of the US for a few years. Mark worked for a number of years as head electronics technician for the DJM music stores, as well as doing broadcast and recording studio engineering and construction. In 1991, Mark and his wife bought a 36-foot sailboat that needed a major electrical overhaul. As Mark was working on that project, other boaters would come over to watch him. Confident that Mark knew what he was doing, the other boaters started asking for help with their own electrical issues. In 1992, Mark raised his sheet and started a side business working on boat electrical systems. In 1994, Mark left the music industry, began Mobile Marine Electrical Services (MMES) Custom Panels, formerly in Newburyport, Massachusetts, now in Salem, New Hampshire, full time, and has never looked back.

Custom Electrical Panels and Wiring Harnesses

Robin: **What are custom electrical and instrumental panels?**

Mark: Custom panels are usually one of a kind, or a very small number of, panels designed to fit specific needs and applications, such as size, shape, number and types of circuits, metering/monitoring, remote controls, and so on. With a custom panel, we can eliminate many of the compromises one must make using a "one-size-fits-all" production panel.

We are a Blue Sea Systems dealer, so if a production panel meets a customer's needs, we can provide that as well. We are one of a handful of dealers authorized by Blue Seas to configure their 360 Series modular custom panels, so we cover all the bases.

In terms of the types of panels we do, everything from a panel with a single switch to very complex multi-voltage panels; small name or label plates to large menu boards for whale watch boats. We've done engine panels, panels to mount electronics displays like radars into, and so on. We do mostly boats, but also some other stuff. A couple of years ago we did a set of three panels, with something like 36 rocker switches on each, for a train that goes around the country spraying herbicides on the railroad bed. We also did the interface boxes and harnesses to all the motorized control valves on that system. That was kind of a neat project.

Robin: Did you go on the train?

Mark: No. Actually, they called a couple of months ago and they're talking about doing another one at some point. I look forward to working on that again.

Robin: **Why would I, as a boater, want a customized panel?**

Mark: If you need to fit a panel into a particular sized space and there is not a production panel made that would fit there; or if you want specific items on your panel that do not come on a production panel, such as an inverter, generator remote, or some other piece of equipment, then you really need a custom panel. You can have much dressier panels than most mass produced ones if you want, with the boat name and/or the boat builder's name, or almost anything else, on it. You can light the panel up for an even cooler look. We can personalize panels as much as you desire. With a custom panel, you can have more options and choice than almost any panel fabricator gives you. Some customers are just looking for a faceplate on which to install their existing engine gauges, since the panel they currently have might be cracked or broken. We can do anything from a blank panel to a fully loaded one with a terminal block back plane and the harness between the two.

Robin: **You mentioned a back plane—what's that?**

Mark: A terminal back plane is a piece of material generally smaller than the panel itself by half an inch or an inch or so, so it'll fit through the same hole. It mounts behind the panel. On the terminal back plane are mounted all the terminal blocks, bus bars, and stuff. Each terminal on the terminal block is labeled as to what device connects there. Then we build a harness between the panel and that assembly. The customer mounts the back plane and the panel, and then all he or she has to do is make connections with wires coming from the various devices on his boat to the back plane. As long as you know what the wires are, it's real easy to hook up.

Robin: Sounds complicated. My head is dizzy.

Mark: Actually, it's pretty easy. The harness between the back plane and the panel is all pre-wired and pre-tested, so you don't have to touch anything there—all the technical wiring is done.

Robin: Are there any differences between a panel for a power boat and one for a sail boat?

Mark: In electrical panels, not usually a lot. For custom panels on sailboats, one thing we do that's a little different than power boats is set up a selector switch for the navigation lights that is fed by a single breaker, rather than having multiple breakers for navigation lights, anchor light, strobe light, and so on. We'll have a single breaker that feeds a small rotary switch. That rotary switch has multiple positions—say, steaming anchored, sailing, and strobe and tri-colored light positions—those are fitted—and you just set the switch to whatever mode you're in. If you're motoring at night, flip it to steaming and it automatically configures the running lights to the proper combination. You don't have to turn on and off different breakers and try to remember which lights are supposed to be on for this—you just hit the switch.

Recreational power boats usually don't have too much—you're either underway or anchored. A pair of breakers works fine in that case. Commercial fishing boats use a number of different combinations of lights, so we can also do the same thing there with a rotary switch automatically configured for whatever mode of fishing they're doing. Engine panels for powerboats are usually more complicated—there are more parameters you're reading on the engines and often there are twin engines rather than a single one—that's more complicated than a typical sailboat engine panel.

Robin: Can a boater take a panel from a salvaged boat and customize it to fit their own boat?

Mark: Not usually. In a rare case I suppose you could, but you don't know what you're getting in terms of quality of the breakers and that kind of stuff. It's sort of like being stuck with a production panel in that the size is what it is and you have to make it fit or hope it fits your space.

With a custom panel, of course, we can make it any size and shape you want. If you want an electrical panel in the shape of an S, we can do that.

Robin: **An interesting wiring conundrum is how do you effectively, and safely to marine standards, connect low power instrument power leads to larger units with heavier power leads; for example, connecting 30 or 32 wiring to AWG 14 or 16 tinned copper stranded wire?**

Mark: Often, for those items, you can provide a single breaker that feeds a fuse block with the requisite number of fuse positions for those devices. That way, each small wire can go to its own terminal on the fuse block. This lets you bring in a larger cable or larger wire like a 14, 16, or 10, depending on how many fuses or the ampage between the breaker and the fuse block. You have low amp fuses for each individual small device and each little wire goes to its own terminal. This lets you get rid of the inline fuse holders found in the power leads of each unit and moves them all to a central location—that's nice. You're not looking for wires wrapped up in a bundle somewhere. For the higher current items like radar, VHF, and single side band (SSB) radios, we generally give each one of those its own breaker. It's the small current stuff for which we'll use a single master breaker.

Robin: **A number of manufacturers now make it possible to connect a PC to a chart plotter to a VHF radio, so we can get navigation software all working together. What does that entail?**

Mark: There are a couple of ways to do those type of connections—you can either use the little 22 sized heat shrink covered butt connectors and just splice the wires together, or you can use something like the Blue Seas #2408 or similar terminal block, with little ring terminals for each one. The advantage to doing it with the ring terminals and the terminal block is that you can move things around and reconfigure if you need to. With the heat shrink butt connection, if you want to change stuff you've got to cut the butt connector off and re-splice. We like the terminal blocks, but it depends on whether you're going to change it in the future.

Robin: So, we've decided as a boater that we want to get a customized panel. Can you walk me through the process of getting one?

Mark: We start by discussing the customer's needs. Sometimes the discussion can be pretty simple and straightforward if he or she only needs a small number of breakers to fit in a given space—maybe a meter or two. If that's the case, we just need to know a few other things such as the style of breakers s/he wants—flat, actuator, or toggle style. Does s/he want indicator lights? Does s/he want the labels backlit or not? We can come up with a pretty quick CAD design and price estimate and send it to the customer as a PDF file. Then they can look at it and decide if the layout is what they like and whether they want to add, change, or delete. We give them that and the price estimate, and they can make a decision at that point. For more complex panels, there are some other things we need to know, so there are a few more questions—what the overall dimensions we have to stay within are, as well as the depth that's available behind the panel face. Then we can talk about the type of circuit breaker panel—is it going to be an A/C panel, a D/C panel, or a combination of both? What voltages will it be controlling—12- or 24-volt D/C, for example, or 120/240volts A/C (maybe 120-volt, 208-volts

6

three-phase A/C on the big yacht, or some combination of the former)? What do you want for metering and monitoring and voltage and currents? We've done panels with as many as four different voltages on them. We did one that had 12- and 24-volt D/C *and* 120-volt A/C *and* 208-volt A/C three-phase on it for a big air conditioning unit. There are a few other questions we ask. What other items are you going to want—a generator and a verter remote, tank level gauges, refrigeration controls, and so on? At that point we can start doing CAD layouts for that and actually see what we need for space, given what they've told us we have to stay within. Next we send the drawing to the customer and get their suggestions and/or approval of the design. If they want to move stuff around, it's still fairly simple at this point, because it's just keystrokes on the computer. Once we start cutting it (laughing), that's what it is, so in the CAD phase is when it's real easy to say, "I want to change this. Can we put the A/C section on top and the D/C on the bottom?" or something like that. But once all that stuff is established, we can talk about the esoteric things: the color of the panel; a single- or multi-layer panel; backlighting on the labels and, if so, what color back lighting; etc. Once we've got most of those questions answered and we've done the layout so we know it's going to fit, then we can start working on pricing. It's pretty much the same for any other type of panel—engine instrument panels, navigational display panels, or whatever. The order in which we ask the questions might change; and there might be some additional questions we ask, or some things we don't need to ask, depending on what the panel is. Of course, we might make some suggestions too, but that's the basic sequence of events.

***Robin:* With electrical plugs, it makes a big difference whether we're here in the US or in the UK, Israel, or down south in the islands. Do you change how you set these panels up depending on where the boat's going to be traveling?**

Mark: In some cases, particularly with the A/C systems on the boat. Here we can use single pole breakers, whereas in the UK, Europe, and a lot of those countries, they have to switch both sides of the A/C line, what we would call hot/neutral, so sometimes the layout is a little bit different there – we'll just use double-hold breakers instead of singles. In most cases, there's not a lot of difference. The meters we use, for example, are digital meters, most of the A/C ones can read voltage up to 300 volts, so they'll work fine on the 120-volt domestic A/C systems and they'll work on the 230-volt European system with no change or modification whatsoever. We've done a couple of panels where we had a selector switch which selected between different windings on a shore power isolation transformer, what they call an international transformer. By changing the way the transformer is tapped or the way the linings are connected, you can change the input and output voltages on it. We would put in two different inlets on the boat, one for US shore power and one for European. All they would have to do is flip the selector switch to reconfigure the transformer for whichever place they were in. It provided the proper voltage out to the panel; from that point it was all pretty much the same thing. That worked out very well.

Robin: That makes a lot of sense and sounds like it's a lot easier to do it that way than to try to remember. **Let's talk about wiring and lights on a boat for a second. When is the best time to replace these?**

Mark: If the wiring is old, with cracked insulation, for example, or the conductors are turning green, black, or crumbling, it's probably a good time to do it. If the wiring's been exposed to salt water, if the boat probably took on water or sat on the bottom or something, I'd recommend it be replaced. Another place you need to look is wiring to the bilge pump. Usually, down in the bilge, it's damp/wet; sometimes the wiring isn't properly supported up out of the water; it sits in it. You want to keep an eye on that and maybe change the wiring when it starts to look like it might be getting water ingress into the wire itself or wicking up the conductors. If the boat was wired using automotive wire, you might consider replacing the wiring; even worse, if the boat was wired with house type wire—solid conductor stuff like you buy at Home Depot—it's basically not legal to use on boats, but I've seen boats wired with it.

Robin: **Why would they be wired with that? Do boats come that way?**

Mark: No. Usually the owner decides to add some wiring. They run over to Home Depot and they're not aware of the requirements for marine electrical systems. They just go and grab some wire and wire nuts and put the thing together. The problem with using single strand solid wire is that vibration causes the wire to flex and crack after a while, whereas the stuff we use is many very thin strands that can flex a lot and not have a problem.

There's been some discussion about tin wire. We use it all the time—it's not a requirement, just another safety factor. You can use stranded un-tin wire, there's no requirement that says you have to use tin, but we don't use anything but.

Another thing: a lot of people pay ridiculously high prices for name brand marine wire, and they're really paying for the name. A lot of it—the stuff we use—is really very high quality wire; the company that makes it, makes a lot of it for the brand name people, but you can buy it for a lot less—that's something to look at if you're looking at rewiring a boat.

Robin: **Now what about connecting the wires together with wire nuts?**

9

Mark: You don't do that on a boat—wire nuts are really designed for house stuff. On boats, wiring must be properly terminated with crimped connectors or a proper type of what they call a Eurostyle terminal block, which has not just a screw that screws down into the wire to hold it, but it's got a little plate the screw pushes down against so it doesn't put the screw down through the wires and crush them.

I meant to mention lighting fixtures, especially lighting fixtures for navigational lights that are outside—the sockets on those are prone to corrosion because water can get into them from time to time, then you start having issues there. A lot of times you find your navigation lights are flickering on and off, getting dimmer, or whatever; if that's the case, then the sockets are going. You can clean them, but you really ought to just replace the fixture because it's only going to get worse over time. There's weird stuff we've seen.

Robin: Every time I go on a boat, I never know what I'm going to see either.

Mark: We had a boat here a couple weeks ago that one of the previous owners had added some stuff to. They'd wired it all with #18 or 20 wire, which is way undersized for the loads they wanted to run; they worked, but barely. They'd gotten into an emergency situation—they had a #18 wire feeding the bilge pump, which really should have been a #12—it helps to know some of the marine codes when you're doing this stuff.

Robin: **You mentioned replacing wires if they have been under salt water. Too many times I've seen trailers end up in the water from inexperienced drivers bringing their boats back on land. In this scenario, how often would you recommend changing the wires?**

Mark: It depends on the wires. A lot of trailers are wired with

SAE (Society of Automotive Engineers) automotive wire, so probably you'll get a couple of years out of it. The biggest thing with trailers is that a lot of the light fixtures—the brake lights and stuff and the little marker lights—aren't water tight. If you back it in, and you didn't disconnect the lights so they're on when you're backing into the water, salt water hitting the connections, sockets, and stuff, becomes conductive and immediately starts generating green conductive crud and starts eating away at the metal there. First thing to do before you back a trailer into the water is unplug it, so you at least don't have electricity flowing through. In a lot of cases, you have no choice but to sink the lights while you're launching your boat or recovering it.

As far as replacing the wire, it depends. If they use high quality wire, the stuff can take repeated submersions because it's not sitting in salt water for long periods of time—so it dries fairly quickly. As long as the water doesn't wick up the wires, it's generally not too big a deal. The thing to do, probably, is if you start having some issues with brake lights and what-not, you can usually loosen a screw and pull the wire out of the connection at the tail light and look at it to see if it's corroding. If it is, try cutting it back an inch or two and see if you can get the clean wire to make a new connection at that point. If it's really corroding and wicking up the wire a fairly good distance, it's probably time to cut the wire out and replace it.

Robin: **I noticed when I was doing some research for our interview there were quite a few places they mentioned ABYC and US Coast Guard Standards. What does ABYC stand for?**

Mark: That's the American Boat and Yacht Council. They're the ones that kind of propagate the rules and regulations on small craft. Basically they're a standard setting organization and a lot of their regulations closely follow the national fire codes, electrical codes, and stuff like that; with, obviously, some changes. Things that we talked about—like not using solid wire, or wire nuts, and stuff—they've come out with. They have a very thick book that basically covers all phases of construction of boats up to 65 feet—there's an electrical section, a fuel section, a section on helm visibility, and that kind of stuff—they're the guys that do that. They work with technical committees, the Coast Guard, the national fire code people, and all that. In there, they'll be charts of wire sizing; voltage drop in various currents and distances of run; and all this other stuff—there's a lot of things that enter into it. We follow all of that.

Robin: **Have they ever been known to check out somebody's boat and inspect it to make sure that it's up to code?**

Mark: I don't think the ABYC does, but the Coast Guard would, because they have law enforcement powers. With the ABYC, their stuff is not really law, it's suggestion. But if you have a problem with your boat, a fire or whatever, and the insurance company finds out you weren't following ABYC standards, then you might have an issue. As far as the ABYC stopping a boat and saying, "We want to search your boat," it wouldn't happen. The Coast Guard, on the other hand, they can do a boarding and check; but they're basically checking for safety equipment—whether the boat is in reasonably good shape, that type of thing; safe to go to sea, so to speak.

Robin: **So it's good to follow the ABYC standards, g-d forbid there's an insurance policy that needs to be acted upon.**

Mark: Yeah, it's all based on safety issues, for the most part. They have a thing that's kind of like a regulation, or whatever you want to call it, for line of sight from the helm—whether you can see safely and that type of thing. It's the same thing with electrical stuff, the fuel systems, and all these various "this is how it should be done" types of things.

Robin: **What type of maintenance program should one have for their panels and wiring harnesses?**

Mark: There is not really a lot of maintenance you can do on them other than keeping them clean, making sure the connections stay tight, and that sort of thing. There's nothing that really wears out or that type of thing. As long as the thing is in normal use, and you don't put it under water, there's not a lot to do to it other than keeping it reasonably clean and making sure the connections aren't loose.

Robin: **How should you clean these panels and harnesses?**

Mark: It depends on what gets on them for dirt. Just a damp rag using Windex or something like that'll work perfectly fine on the materials we use. I would suggest you turn the power off to the panel. Even if you're cleaning the front of it, it's probably not a bad idea. As far as behind the panel, about the only thing you really do is look for loose connections and that type of thing. In general, there's not going to be much issue. If dust and dirt get back there, vacuum it out; beyond that, there's not a lot to do.

Robin: **Is it good to clean them at the end of the day when you're done sailing or boating?**

Mark: No. Unless it's getting splashed by seawater or something, which shouldn't happen—an engine panel up at the helm or in the cockpit or something might take a spray every once in a while—but as far as the D/C breaker panel, the A/C breaker panel, that's generally in protected places anyway. Once a year give them a quick clean—open it up and take a look at the connections; disconnect power to the boat and shut the batteries off before you do it—other than that, there's really not much to do.

Robin: **Do they need to coat all the connections with any dielectric material to prevent corrosion?**

Mark: If the connections are in a place where they tend to get some salt moisture, it's probably not a bad idea. Giving them a spray of that type of protectant once a year, when you're commissioning the boat, is probably not a bad idea. If they're in places like up under a fly bridge, underneath the dash panel, and stuff, things probably tend to get damper because it's a bit more open. Up there, you probably would want to spray the terminal blocks with some type of dielectric and keep them clean. Also, it's probably a good idea to get in there every once in a while and vacuum that out, particularly before you're spraying because otherwise you're just capturing all the dust and dirt, holding it in place.

Robin: **When's the best time to replace the wiring on these panels?**

Mark: If the wire's showing signs of being cracked or corroded, has been exposed to excessive heat, or has been underwater—you'd want to replace it. What's the best time? When the boat's undergoing a major refit and a lot of the equipment's been removed and you can get at the wiring. Invariably, a lot of wiring is hidden away in tough to get at spots. I know on our boat, when we were rewiring it the first time, it was just a nightmare. A lot of the wiring had actually been glassed in along the hull, so you couldn't get to it. You had to cut the wire where it disappeared under the glass, cut it where it came out again, and run a new wire through a conduit, behind a settee, or something like that. The more accessible it is, the easier it is.

Robin: **How about the boaters replacing these panels themselves, can they do it?**

Mark: Yeah, they can. As long as they have basic marine electrical systems knowledge and a few tools, it shouldn't be all that difficult to take the old panel out and wire a new one in. One thing we highly recommend is a good pair of ratchety crimpers, though. With the $10 ones you get when you buy a package of crimp connectors, after you've done about 10 or 15 crimps you're going to find that your hand doesn't have the strength to crimp them properly. With ratcheting crimpers, once you start to squeeze them, they won't release until you've applied the proper pressure to the crimps, so you know you've always got a good connection. The problem with the cheap ones is that half the time you give a tug on the connector and it comes right off the wire—that's not a good thing.

The customer can replace it themselves as I said with a little bit of electrical knowledge. One of the things we do actually makes it easier for a lot of panel installations, and I don't know of any other panel company that does it, is we'll build a terminal block backplane and harness assembly that goes with the panel. We do that for probably close to 75% of our customers these days. Basically, it's what we discussed a little earlier—a piece of material that's got all the terminal blocks and bus bars and stuff mounted to that, and it's all engraved with everything labeled as to what it is, and a prewired and pretested harness between it and the panel. This whole thing is, essentially, a single unit. You mount the panel and mount the backplane, and you just make your connections, each one where it says to go on the backplane, and you're pretty much done with it. That helps a lot. There's no other wiring that goes to the panel or anything—we've premade that harness; it's all pretested; all the real technical wiring is right there and we've done it all already. If you've got a volt meter with a selector switch to read three batteries, we've got three terminals there labeled 'Battery 1,' 'Battery 2,' 'Battery 3,' and you just connect right to those. You're not doing stuff up on the panel or any place that's the real technical difficult stuff—it's all done; it's all tested and we know it all works. It eliminates an awful lot of headache for the boat owners. And you don't need a schematic or anything or to be an electrical technician to do it—if you can use basic hand tools, cutters, strippers, crimpers, and a screwdriver, you can do the installation yourself.

Robin: **What if they decided they didn't want to do the installation themselves?**

Mark: You can either find somebody who's knowledgeable about marine electrical work or, ideally, find an ABYC-certified marine electrical technician to mount it and wire it up for you.

Robin: **Let's talk for a minute about a boater upgrading their instrument panel—how would they do that?**

Mark: For some customers it's as simple as making a new faceplate. They install their existing gauges, switches, and so on, as long as those things are in good shape; maybe the panel is cracked, or broken, but the gauges and switches all work. We can make them a new faceplate; they just put it together and put it back the way it was electrically; it looks nice and new, and they're all set to go. Maybe they're changing the boat or they want to change the color of the panel, update it or something. We do some double-layer panels—which is essentially the base panel, which is the full size of the panel, with all the holes for breakers, switches, lights, labels, and that stuff; then we can do sort of a bezel overlay just around the outside or setting off different areas of the panel—the overlay could be a different color than the base panel layer is. It makes for some neat, kind of dressy looking panels to do it that way.

Robin: **They can get as fancy as they want or keep it as plain as they want.**

Mark: Yup—we can do anything from a real utilitarian lobster boat looking panel to a megayacht looking panel, and almost anything in between.

Robin: **What type of warranty can they expect with a customized panel?**

Mark: Well, for us, generally, it's 90 or 180 days. If something fails on the panel with normal usage, we'll usually repair it or replace it. If it's been obviously abused, we may decline to do that—if somebody's whacked the panel with a hammer, for example, or sunk it. In most cases, if a breaker or a meter or something in normal use goes bad, we'll supply them with a new one. Because we use high quality parts, generally we don't have too many issues like that.

Robin: **Batteries seem to be a sore point with a lot of boaters. How long do the batteries last and can boaters replace the batteries themselves?**

Mark: They can. Generally, if you're buying a kind of run of the mill generic battery, three or four years would be the average lifespan. If you're buying a good premium type battery—like a Rolls or something like that—and you have a good, well-regulated charging system, your batteries could last...I've seen them last ten years or more. In most cases you can replace a battery yourself, as long as you put the positive wires back on the positive terminal and negative wires on the negative terminal, and you can lift a heavy battery, because some of them aren't light. I've got a large house battery in my boat that weighs 162 pounds—I was wrestling that around this morning, as a matter of fact.

Robin: **What about using aftermarket batteries? Is this a case where straight from the manufacturer batteries work best and you should shy away from aftermarket?**

Mark: We prefer to use a more premium type of battery, although there are some inexpensive aftermarket batteries that are not bad. It's sort of out of our field of what we do.

Robin: **Are there any known cases where an aftermarket battery caused a problem?**

Mark: I'm certain there are. I was trying to remember back when we were doing boats. It seems to me we had a case or two where the owner had inexpensive batteries that they grabbed at some discount house or something like that, and they wouldn't hold a charge or that type of thing, but you can get that in anything. We found that, generally, you get what you pay for—if you buy a premium battery, you get premium lifetime out of it.

Robin: **I've seen on some panels that there are different colors. Is there significance to the colors?**

Mark: Not really—it's more of an aesthetic thing. If we were doing an emergency panel, particularly on a commercial boat, we might make that out of red as a function of what the panel is. For the most part, it's a question of what looks good where the panel will be mounted. Does it look better in black, white, carbonate fiber? It's really a customer's choice. We do a number of colors.

Robin: **Can you get these materials engraved?**

Mark: Oh, yeah. Most of the panels we do are either surface engraving—where you're looking at, say, a white panel with a black core, so anything we engrave looks black and the surface is white; or we're doing what we call reverse engraving, where the panel itself is clear—typically an eighth inch acrylic—and then the back side of that has a 10 or 15 thousandths of an inch thick film in whatever color you want to see—typically either matte black, dark gray, or something like that. Then we engrave on the back side, but we engrave everything reversed, so that when you're looking through it from the front of the panel, it looks proper. Then we can paint fill that engraving in virtually any color, or we can backlight it, which is how we do our labels. They're a sixteenth of an inch thick reverse engraved acrylic, and then we backlight it in red, green, blue, white, amber. We had one panel we did with a little rocker switch on it that selected between white and red backlighting—the customer used white in the day time, so it stood out, and at night he went to red.

Robin: **Red's not hard to see at night?**

Mark: Oh no, red's actually real good at night—it preserves your night vision.

Robin: **What's a color that you see a lot?**

Mark: The two colors we use most would be black with white lettering or white with black lettering. Right now we seem to be doing a lot of panels where the base panel layer is the carbon fiber print look and then either a burl wood bezel or black bezel around it. We're doing some where the panel itself is a burl look with black bezel, but black and white are still the most popular colors.

Robin: **Have you done any in what you thought would be bizarre colors that actually turned out to be pretty nice?**

Mark: I can't think of anything that we've done that was bizarre.

Robin: Wait 'til I get my boat.

Mark: Actually, we did a couple of switch panels for a guy in

Michigan—nice guy, too; we'd done some work for him before—he wanted a textured blue; he was matching a couple of decorative panels at the helm and he wanted two switch panels that would match that. So we got some blue textured material with a white core, engraved it, made two switch panels out of it, and it actually did look pretty cool.

Robin: **What's the difference between a panel and wiring harness?**

Mark: The panel has all the circuit breakers, switches, meters, and components on it. The harness is the bundle of wires that runs between the panel and the terminal block backplane if there is a terminal block backplane, or from panel out to all the boat devices, if there isn't a backplane. It's like a wiring harness in a car, same idea.

Robin: I never thought of my car as having a wiring harness.

Mark: Oh yeah! Actually, it's a pretty complex one.

Robin: **What's a clever way to repair the rubber sleeve protector on an outboard external wiring harness?**

Mark: What we've done there is taken what is called split loomed tubing—it comes in various diameters and, essentially, looks like a piece of corrugated hose, but it's split length wise—you just open it up, wrap that around the existing wiring harness, and secure the two ends with hose clamps or cable tie wraps or something like that.

It does a pretty good job of protecting your wiring harness. We actually use that stuff a lot on the harnesses we make between the panel and the backplane. The other thing we use a lot now is what they call expandable sleeve tubing. It's braided tubing—if you push down on it lengthwise, the diameter on it expands; if you pull it, like pulling on a rope, it gets smaller in diameter and tightens up—it'll fit almost any size wiring harness. It comes in various what they call standard sizes—I think they start at three-eighths of an inch and go up to maybe an inch and a half or bigger. It makes for a really neat-looking installation and keeps everything all bundled together nicely.

Robin: **If someone's having problems with their boat trailer lights, where should they start to diagnose the problem?**

Mark: The first thing to do is check your tow vehicle's fuses. There are fuses for brake lights and all the different circuits. If you're lucky, all you've done is popped a fuse. Generally the fuse block is under the hood or perhaps under the dashboard—it depends on your particular vehicle. That's the first place I would look. Then take a look at the trailer connector where it plugs into the car or pickup, whatever you're towing with. Sometimes they'll get wet and corrode—if they're wet and there's electricity flowing through them, it tends to generate corrosion. Past that, I would check the tail light sockets and the sockets with various bulbs on the trailer. But check the fuses first, because that's the easiest thing to fix.

Robin: **Is there any way to protect these sockets so they last a little longer?**

Mark: If it's not a water tight tail light; and most often they're not, apparently; you can put some dielectric grease on them and insert the bulb into the socket. That'll help, at least for a while.

Robin: **If someone needs a schematic for a wiring harness, can they call you?**

Mark: They can, if it's a harness that we built, then, obviously, we can provide them with a schematic. If it's a harness for a production boat, your best bet probably is to go online, do a search for the make and model of the boat and wiring harness. The other thing is that a lot of times there are user groups for various boat manufacturers, like a Sea Ray users group, a Bayliner® users group, and so on—a lot of times those guys can be a font of information; can tell you where you can find that kind of information. We don't generally have that stuff here, although if somebody wants to give us a call we'd be more than happy to see if we could locate the information for them.

Robin: What type of information would you need from someone before they call, say they're looking for a schematic?

Mark: We'd need to know the make, model, and year of the boat; and what particular piece of equipment schematic they're looking for. Are they looking for the whole boat wiring diagram, an engine harness diagram, and so on? The more information they have, the more it helps us get a direction to go in, to give *them* a direction to go in.

Robin: Any other suggestions on whom else they can call?

Mark: If you're looking for an engine wiring diagram, try calling the engine manufacturer. You could call a dealer for that type of engine—they have service manuals and they can make a copy of a schematic for you or tell you where you can get one. Again, users groups are a pretty good way to find out that stuff. The other day I was looking for something else and came across a users group for old outboard motors. They had a bunch of old schematics, stuff that wasn't generally available; someone just collected the stuff over the years and had a little library of it.

Robin: That's good to know. I would think, too, that if they belong to any yacht clubs or have access to boat yards and maybe marinas would have stuff.

Mark: Boat yards, usually, if they're a dealer for, say, Yamaha outboards or Johnson motors or something like that, they would usually have a pretty good set of manuals for those things and generally I would expect that you could get schematics and parts lists and that sort of stuff from them.

Robin: **Let's talk for a minute about things changing in the future, as they always do. Are there any new standards that are coming up that boaters need to be aware of as far as electrical?**

Mark: As far as the electrical stuff goes, I know the ABYC is coming out with a new standard for what they call ELCIs (equipment leakage circuit interrupters), which are going to start being required on boats. They were actually supposed to start last year, but because of shortages in the industry, you couldn't get some of the equipment that was going to be required. Some of the bigger ELCIs, like the 50-amp and 100-amp units, just aren't readily available. So they moved that back to, I think it's, July 31st of this year. Basically, what that is, if you're familiar with the GFI outlets in your house—which trip if there's an electrical leakage or grounding problem or something—those protect whatever's plugged into them, that piece of equipment. What they're requiring now is one that will protect the whole boat electrical system, because the regular outlet ones don't protect things like a hardwired water heater, an air conditioner unit, that type of thing. So now they're requiring something that protects all the electrical systems on the boat.

Robin: **Does this have anything to do with a safety precaution for fires on the boats?**

Mark: Not so much fires, that's over-current protection. This is for electrical leakage or people getting shocks or getting electrocuted, that type of thing. It's more of a human safety type of thing than equipment overload. Basically, what they say is, and I'll read this, "ABYC regulation E 13.3.5 states, if installed in a head, galley, machinery space, or on the weather deck, the receptacle shall be protected by a Type A nominal 5 milliampere ground fault circuit interrupter (GFCI)."[1] These are usually the familiar GFCI outlets like you see in your house, which protect against flaws—against devices plugged into them—but don't protect from a failing hardwired device, such as a water heater. "ELCI units are required to be installed within 10 feet of the shore power inlet and offer ground fault protection for the entire A/C shore power system beyond the ELCI unit itself." That's actually off the Blue Sea Systems website. If your listeners want more detailed information, I suggest they go to the Blue Sea Systems website—www.BlueSea.com—there's a wealth of excellent information on electric marine design and equipment there. Anyway, that's the biggest change that I'm aware of at this point that's coming down the road. That probably doesn't affect most boaters in terms of what they're doing, it affects boat builders, because they have to start putting that equipment on. Obviously, if boaters want to upgrade their existing electrical systems to include that it is not a bad idea.

Robin: **Is that an expensive proposition?**

Mark: They're not inexpensive devices. I'm trying to remember off the top of my head what the 30 amp one goes for.

Robin: **Nothing on a boat is inexpensive.**

Mark: It is a good piece of safety gear, so I guess in that regard, it's relatively inexpensive compared to saving somebody's life. I

---

[1]

http://bluesea.com/files/resources/technical_briefs/Technical_Brief_AC_Ground_Faults.pdf don't know what the price is going to be on the 50- and 100-amp ones. The 30-amp ones, if I remember correctly, retail for $175 or something like that (don't quote me because I'm talking off the top of my head). I'm sure the larger ones will cost more. Again, it's a real good investment, because people get electrocuted every year on boats or if there's an electrical leakage on the boat and it's getting to the prop shaft and metal parts underwater and somebody's swimming around the docks, there's been cases where people have been electrocuted because of a faulty electrical system on the boat and they weren't even touching the boat.

Robin: That brings up a good point. When I owned my house, I actually grounded the house in case of an electrical storm. **Is this something similar? I know there have been boaters that have lost their boats because lightning has struck the mast and away the boat goes. Is this going to help protect them for that as well?**

Mark: No—this is protecting against electrical power leakage faults. Basically, what it's doing is it's looking at the hot wire and it's looking at the neutral wire and the A/C shore power system and if the current coming down the hot wire is not exactly the same as the current going back to the neutral wire, within 30 milliamps, this thing says, "Wait a minute, that current that's 30 milliamps less coming back the neutral wire than was going down the hot wire, that's going somewhere it shouldn't— I'm shutting the system off." But, as far as lightning hitting the boat, no, it won't help that at all.

Robin: But that's extra current. We're not going to get into this discussion, because I could go for hours with that one.

Mark: It may well trip the unit if it doesn't blow it up from the voltage spike, but lightning is a whole different issue. In that case, you want—and there's a whole argument there about whether you should bond a boat or not bond a boat—well, that's for galvanic corrosion. Our boat was hit by lightning as a matter of fact—three years ago?—lightning hit the top of the mast and pretty much wiped out everything electrical on it.

Robin: I've actually met somebody whose boat caught on fire from being hit by lightning. It's scary.

Mark: A lot of times, if lightning hits the boat, it'll find a place to exit somewhere under water—often times that place is something like a through-hull transducer or something for the depth sounder—and just blows it right out of the boat and then the boat sinks. We were lucky in that regard—some of it exited through the through-hull, but it didn't blow it out of the boat; but it wiped out an awful lot of electronics.

Robin: I understand you have clients all over the world. How does that work?

Mark: It works pretty much the same as if we had a client a state away. Almost everything we do is done via the internet, some phone calls, but most of it's done via the website. We have a ton of pictures on our website and people can see those and see all the various configurations that we've done and get ideas. We email drawings back and forth. Customers send us questions, comments, and suggestions. We send them questions, comments, and suggestions. As we described earlier, the process of how we come up with a design—it doesn't matter if somebody's 50 miles away or 5,000 miles away. In fact, DHL just came about an hour ago and picked up 10 panel faceplates that are going to Australia. We'll never see the boat other than some photographs once they're installed. We never meet the owners. There's lots of emails back and forth.

Robin: Any other tips you want to give boaters on customizing their electrical or instrument panels?

Mark: Think about any additions or changes you might want to make in the future and design for those eventualities now. For example, if you are thinking of adding an inverter in the future, you can design for that, so that when you do install it, all you need to do is remove a couple of jumpers, make the connections to the inverter, and you're off and running. We always try to design in 15-20% of the total number of breakers as spares at the time the panel is being built. Somebody's always going to find something to add even if they go, "Nope, I've got everything I want." Next year some new toy will come out and, "I've got to have that," or they want to add another light someplace or something like that. If you're getting a new panel built, try to think of everything, if you think you know everything you're going to want to put on it now, leave space for a couple more items you might add to the boat's electrical system as time goes on.

Robin: Any last comments on wiring harnesses?

Mark: We highly recommend if you have a custom panel built, or even if you're buying a production panel from us like one of the Blue Sea's panels, have us build a backplane and harness for it. Unless you're really, really knowledgeable about doing the electrical, or you have somebody doing it for you, if we can make a harness and a backplane, it makes things so much easier. As far as harnessing for the rest of the boat, we can do that as well, as long as we have all the pertinent information, or, even better, if you can tear out the old harness and send it to us, we can copy lengths, connectors, and all that stuff. And send a bunch of notes in terms of stuff you're adding and where it's going to be in the boat, so we can put in the wires for those. We don't travel to work on boats any more—we used to—but if the boat can come to us at our facility we'll be happy to work on it.

Robin: **Where is your facility located?**

Mark: If people want to take a look at what we do, see our website: www.WeWireBoats.com.

Note: Since this interview was conducted, Mark's company name and location have changed. He is now at MMES Custom Panels, 28 School Street, Salem, NH 03079. He can be reached by email at MMESCustomPanels@aol.com, by phone at 603-890-1723, and by fax at 603-890-1728.

Closing
Robin: Mark, I want to thank you for being generous with your time today. You've given me, and probably most of us on the call, a lot of insight regarding custom electrical panels, wire harnessing, and lots of other things.

Mark: I hope I haven't introduced more confusion. Thank you so much for giving me the opportunity to discuss what we do. It's been a real pleasure talking with you. We're a niche business, and not a lot of people know about us or what we do. We appreciate the opportunity to make ourselves known.

Key Points

-- Custom panels for a sailboat can have a selector switch for the navigation lights that is fed by a single breaker.

-- To connect a PC to a chart plotter to a VHF radio, use something like the Blue Sea #2408 or similar terminal block with little ring terminals for each connection.

-- To be able to switch between US and European shore power, install two different inlets on your boat and a selector switch to reconfigure the transformer.

-- You know it's time to replace the wiring on your boat when you see cracked insulation; the conductors are turning green, black, or crumbling; or if the wiring has been exposed to salt water and/or the navigation lights aren't working properly. Check the wiring in the bilge pump. Using automotive wire or, worse, housing wire, is illegal.

-- Make sure wires are properly terminated with crimped connectors or a proper type of Eurostyle terminal blocks.

-- Follow ABYC (American Boat and Yacht Council) guidelines. They are a standard-setting organization and many of their regulations closely follow national fire and electrical codes.

--To prevent corrosion, spray wires with a dielectric protectant once a year when you're commissioning the boat.

--Generic batteries last an average of three to four years. With premium batteries, like Rolls, plus well-regulated charging systems, the battery could last ten years or more.

--A clever way to repair the rubber sleeve protector on an outboard external wiring harness is to open up a piece of split-loomed tubing, wrap it around the existing wiring harness, and secure the two ends with hose clamps or cable tie wrap.

-- Think about any add-ons or changes you might want to make in the future and design for those eventualities now.

Notes

Other Books
If you enjoyed this book, then you'll love...

Buying a Boat, Captain Chris Kourtakis

Marine Surveys, Rob Scanlan

Insuring a Boat, Mike Smith

Financing a Boat Purchase, Jim Coburn

Rent Your Boat, Brian Stefka

Search and Rescue, Alan Sorum

Bad Storms/Heavy Weather, Timothy Wyand

Digital Selective Calling (DSC), the Automatic
Identification System (AIS), and Automated Radio Checks
(ARC), Captain Chris Kourtakis

Multihulls, Jim Brown

Custom Electrical Panels and Wiring Harnesses, Mark
Rogers

Making a Living as a Professional Sailor, Brian Hancock

Seven Tips for a Successful Sale of Your Used Boat, Robin
G. Coles

4 Essential Steps to Buying Your Boat

Boating Secrets: 127 Top Tips to Help You Buy and/or
Enjoy Your Boat, print copy (8.5" x 11", 230 pages)

Or, go to: Boating Secrets Website
(http://BoatingSecrets127TopTips.com) for all our books,
audios, and transcripts

Robin G. Coles

Acknowledgements

Life is full of challenges. Believe me when I say I've had more than my share. But I truly believe that everything happens for a reason—good or bad. Not that one necessarily asks for the bad things to happen.

Only after having my life turned upside down—starting in June 2000, when I was misdiagnosed with MS, and then learning, a year later, that I had cancer and wasn't likely to live ten more years—did I decide it was time to live life and not sweat the small stuff so much like I used to. So here I am writing this acknowledgement and the first two people I'd like to thank are my doctors, Dr. Michael Britt and Dr. Kenneth Miller, for keeping me healthy. It wasn't easy.

This decision took me to learn to sail, travel Europe more, and visit over 300 marinas in the US and abroad. It was an assignment gone wrong that turned out TheNauticalLifestyle.com and this book. But I'm glad I was given that opportunity. Thank you to everyone I've met and spoken with in the marine industry, you have all widened my horizons in one way or another.

To Jim Brown it seems like only yesterday we were juggling our schedules to do this interview. Your willingness to give of your time and knowledge for this project is truly appreciated and I thank you from the bottom of my heart. I wish you all much success.

Others I'd like to thank are Fifi Ball and Marjory Thomas, my writing buddies for five plus years. Their encouragement and tweaking of my articles really helped. Especially Fifi for taking the recording transcripts and turning them into a readable work.

And Mark Hendricks, his countless hours of phone support as this project took on a life of its own.

I would be remiss if I didn't mention my aunt, Dorie Shoer, and my boys Joshua and Lincoln Sziranko, who would throw my words, "Go for it" back at me when I talked about this project. Last but not least, thanks to my best friend George Ryder for encouraging me to follow my dreams and opening up my world. I love you guys!

About the Author

Robin G. Coles is a passionate marine enthusiast and sailor who has interviewed countless industry experts as well as visited, interviewed personnel at, written about, and photographed hundreds of marine ports in the US and abroad.

The ocean both scares and exhilarates her, as it should any boater – one minute it is as calm and smooth as glass; the next a stark raving maniac, as crazy as life itself.

Though Robin has had many challenges in her life, she has always managed to bounce back. Her time on the ocean has been her most rewarding.

Robin has authored a newspaper column and a variety of articles, newsletters, case studies, reports, and technical documents about boating and non-boating topics.

Robin has been a shutterbug from as far back as she can remember. Her photographs have been featured on the cover of the 2008 Winthrop Phonebook, at the 2009 IPEVO show in Las Vegas, and on a local real estate website. To see/read her boating related media, go to www.TheNauticalLifestyle.com/TransientTalk. Her non-boating related media can be found at www.RGColesAndCo.com. Photography can be found at www.NauticalLife.SmugMug.com.

In Robin's spare time she loves to walk the beach, photograph a variety of subjects, read good detective stories, travel, cook, crochet hats for preemie babies and shawls for four-to-six year olds in cancer wards, write, and sail Boston Harbor.

Robin lives on a peninsula near Boston Harbor and Logan Airport, where she sails and works with business owners around the world via satellite phone and internet.

Robin G. Coles

Contact Information

Robin G. Coles
P O Box 520461
Winthrop, MA 02152

339-532-8334

robin@TheNauticalLifestyle.com

Facebook: www.facebook.com/TheNauticalLifestyle

Twitter: www.twitter.com/NauticalLife

Website: www.TheNauticalLifestyle.com

Blog: www.TheNauticalLifestyle.com/TransientTalk

Photographs: www.NauticalLife.SmugMug.com

Non-boating related articles/website:
www.RGColesAndCo.com

Youtube: www.YouTube.com/colesrg

LinkedIn: www.linkedin.com/in/robingcoles/

Robin G. Coles

www.ingramcontent.com/pod-product-compliance
Lightning Source LLC
Chambersburg PA
CBHW071644040426
42452CB00009B/1756